50198117

W9-BUY-041

TELL ME WHY, TELL ME HOW

HOW DO SPIDERS MAKE WEBS?

MELISSA STEWART

 **Marshall Cavendish**
Benchmark
New York

Marshall Cavendish Benchmark
99 White Plains Road
Tarrytown, NY 10591-5502

www.marshallcavendish.us

Library of Congress Cataloging-in-Publication Data

Stewart, Melissa.
  How do spiders make webs? / by Melissa Stewart.
      p. cm.—(Tell me why, tell me how)
  Summary: "Provides comprehensive information on spiders and the process of how they make webs"—Provided by publisher.
  Includes index.
  ISBN 978-0-7614-2920-3
  1. Spider webs—Juvenile literature. 2. Spiders—Juvenile literature.
I. Title. II. Series.

  QL458.4.S75 2009
  595.4'4—dc22

  2007025092

Photo research by Candlepants Incorporated

Cover Photo: Drr.Net / Digital Railroad.net

The photographs in this book are used by permission and through the courtesy of:
Peter Arnold Inc.: George Gornacz /Wwi, 1; Andy Newman/Wwi, 4; Hans Pfletschinger, 12, 20; Paul Springett, 15. Getty Images: Claus Meyer, 5. Photo Researchers Inc.: Paul Whitten, 6; Andrew Syred, 7; Steve Gschmeissner, 19; Perennou Nuridsany, 25; Dr. Samuel Zschokke, 26; Martin Dohrn, 16. Corbis: Dk Limited, 8; Michael & Patricia Fogden, 14; Laurie Chamberlain, 18; Gary W. Carter, 21; Wolfgang Kaehler, 22; Klaus Hackenberg/Zefa, 24. Minden Pictures: Duncan Mcewan/Npl, 9. Digital Railroad.net: Rocco Chilelli/Mira.Com/Drr.Net, 10. Jupiter Images: Robert Llewellyn, 11; Gary Lewis, 17.

Editor: Joy Bean
Publisher: Michelle Bisson
Art Director: Anahid Hamparian
Series Designer: Alex Ferrari

Printed in Malaysia
3 5 6 4 2

CONTENTS

Most spiders are very small, but the Mexican kneed tarantula is large enough to catch mice and small lizards.

What Is a Spider?

You see a tiny creature crawling across the ground. It must be an insect. Right?

Wrong. It could be a spider or a mite or a tick. It could even be a scorpion. All these little critters belong to a group of animals called **arachnids.**

A scorpion is closely related to spiders. It has eight legs and two main body parts.

An insect's body has three main parts—a head, a **thorax**, and an **abdomen**. All adult insects have six legs, two large eyes, and two antennae. Most have four wings and can fly.

An arachnid's body is different. It has two main body parts—a **cephalothorax** and an abdomen. All arachnids have eight legs and special body parts for catching and eating **prey**. They have many eyes, but no wings and no antennae.

This photo clearly shows a spider's cephalothorax (where the legs are attached), abdomen (round area), and eight legs.

What makes spiders different from other arachnids? Every spider has between two and six **spinnerets** on the

underside of its abdomen. These tiny tubelike structures release silk made inside the spider's body.

A close-up view of five spinnerets.

This spider lived long ago in New Zealand. It died when it was trapped in the sticky sap of a kauri tree. Over time, the sap dried and hardened into this piece of golden amber.

Super Spinners

The first spiders probably lived on Earth about 400 million years ago. By about 200 million years ago, spiders living all over the world were building webs. But long before that, spiders were using silk in many other ways.

Many scientists think that spiders first used silk to wrap their eggs. The tough, strong threads helped keep spider eggs safe from birds, frogs, and other hungry **predators**. As time passed, spiders began using silk to build nests and as safety lines to escape from enemies. Eventually, they learned to use silk to catch and wrap prey.

This female candy-stripe spider has wrapped her eggs in a large ball of protective silk.

As spiders developed new ways to use silk, they also developed different kinds of silk. Some kinds, or **species**, of spiders can produce as many as seven different types of silk. Each type does a specific job.

Dragline silk is dry, stiff, and super strong. It helps spiders drop out of sight when an enemy gets too close. Why is it so

This large, colorful Argiope spider has just finished wrapping an insect in silk.

important for spiders to have a way to escape quickly? Even though spiders have up to eight eyes, most cannot see objects clearly. Without a dragline, these spiders would be an easy target for predators.

When this spider senses danger, it spins out a dragline and quickly drops out of site.

Spiders use stretchy silk to build the basic support structure of their webs. Because this silk can stretch to almost twice its original length, it has no problem holding up on windy days. A web also bounces back when a fast-flying insect hits it.

Spiders use thick, sticky threads to build the parts of their webs that will snag and hold prey. The silk they use to wrap

This photo shows a close-up view of a spider pulling silk out of its spinneret.

prey and to protect eggs is dry and strong.

Even though spider silk can be used in many different ways, it is all made of the same basic ingredient—**fibroin**. When fibroin is inside a spider's body, it is a liquid. But as a spider pulls fibroin out of its spinnerets, it changes into long, strong strands.

Now I Know!

Spiders use silk in at least how many different ways?

Four

Many kinds of spiders blend in with their surroundings. But this colorful spider is easy to spot. It has built its web among the flowers of a squash plant.

Why Spiders Make Webs

No one knows exactly how many different kinds of spiders live on Earth. So far, scientists have identified more than 38,000 different species. But there may be many more.

Spiders are **carnivores**, or meat eaters. Most spiders target insects and other small creatures. But some species can catch small fish, small birds, or mice. A few spiders even eat each other.

Scientists divide spiders into two groups based on how they hunt. Web spiders build webs and use them to catch prey. Garden, black widow, and house spiders belong to this group. These spiders also use

A small insect has just flown into this spider's web. The hungry hunter is dashing over to paralyze its prey.

their webs to detect enemies and other spiders. Sometimes they mate and lay eggs on a web. Some spiders even get the water they need by drinking dew off their webs.

Ground spiders catch food without the help of a web. Tarantulas, wolf spiders, and jumping spiders stalk their prey and then chase it down. Trap-door spiders and crab spiders sit and wait for prey to come to them.

About half of all spiders use webs to catch prey. Building a web takes time and energy, but it is worth the effort. A well-built web traps more than 90 percent of the insects that fly into it.

A jumping spider does not use a web to catch prey.

The instant something touches a web, the silk threads start to **vibrate**, or shake. The vibrations tell the spider the size and shape of the intruder. If a leaf or a tiny twig has hit the web, the spider will not react. If an enemy has caused the shaking, the spider flees to safety. But if a helpless insect has flown into the web, the spider attacks.

As the hunter bites the prey with its sharp fangs, a poisonous liquid flows into the insect's body. Within seconds, the prey is either dead or paralyzed. The spider quickly wraps the insect in layer after layer of silk.

If the spider has eaten recently, it will save the food for later. But if the spider is hungry, it chews a hole in the insect's tough outer covering. Then it spits up juices that break down the insect's insides. A few minutes later, the spider slurps up the mushy mixture.

This close-up of a spider's fangs shows how sharp they are.

17

Two spiders have built orb webs side by side on a bush.

Kinds of Spiderwebs

Spiderwebs come in many different sizes and shapes. Some are neatly built, while others are a jumbled mess. Some are flat, while others are bowl-shaped. They can be shaped like a circle or a triangle or even a square.

The largest webs are built by the largest spiders. Webs with the tightest weave are designed to catch very small prey.

Scientists believe that the earliest web builders made

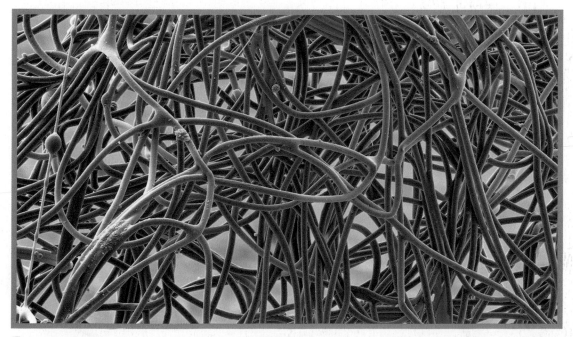

This photo provides a close-up view of a spider's silk.

messy webs near the ground. Today, these **tangled webs** are usually found in dark places, such as under rocks or in the corners of basements. The silk is not sticky, but these webs still do their job. The jumbled maze of threads confuses the prey, so it cannot escape.

Many different kinds of spiders build **sheet webs**. You have probably seen these small, flat webs in the grass or along the tops of bushes. Sheet webs are good for catching hopping insects. Some spiders build a maze of crisscrossing threads above their sheet webs. When an insect collides with one of these lines, it drops down into the web.

A spider built this sheet web in a grassy area. One end is suspended from a wildflower.

A **funnel web** is a sheet web with a funnel-shaped structure in the center or along one edge of the web. The spiders that build funnel webs spend most of their time hiding inside the funnel. When an insect gets trapped in one of these webs, the spider drags the insect inside the funnel and eats its meal in safety.

The funnel usually has two openings. One end opens onto the web's surface. The other end opens below the web and

A spider hides inside the funnel at the center of its thick, messy web.

serves as an emergency exit. Over time, a spider makes its funnel thicker and broader. A spider may spend its whole life on the same funnel web.

Orb webs do not last nearly as long as funnel webs. Most of the time, they have to be rebuilt every day. But the old silk

A spider sits in the middle of its orb web and waits for prey.

strands do not go to waste. Spiders eat the threads and use the **nutrients** in them to live and grow and make new silk.

Scientists believe that orb webs are built by spiders that have lived on Earth for about 136 million years. These complicated, circular webs are usually located high above the ground. They span the open spaces between bushes and trees and are perfect for trapping insects as they whiz through the air.

Now I Know!

Name the four kinds of webs spiders build.

Tangled webs, sheet webs, funnel webs, orb webs.

Its hard to believe that some spiders can build something as complicated as this orb web in as little as thirty minutes.

How Do Spiders Make Webs?

Even though orb webs are complicated, some spiders can build them in as little as thirty minutes. Once a spider has found a good spot for its web, it spins a silk thread and attaches one end to a tree or bush. It lets the other end flutter in the breeze until it catches on something. The entire web will soon hang from this **bridge line**.

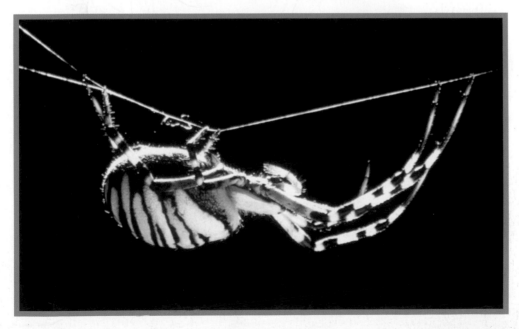

An Argiope spider hangs from a strong, stretchy bridge line.

The spider walks back and forth along the bridge line, spinning out silk to make the line thicker and tighter. Then it lets out a long thread that droops down in the shape of a U.

The spider moves down to the center of the U and attaches a new line. Then the spider drops until it lands on a solid surface. It attaches the thread to this **anchor point** to create a Y-shaped framework.

After crawling back to the center of the framework, the spider begins

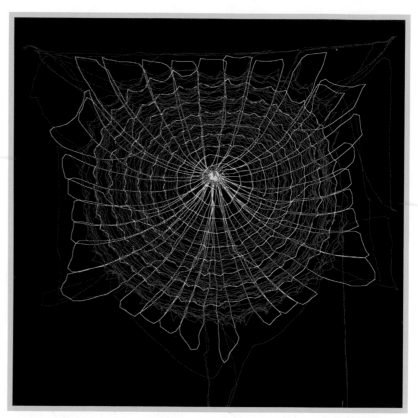

The colors on this image show a spider's movements as it built its orb web. First, the spider laid down the red threads, including the bridge line and the outer framework. Then it spun the yellow threads, which run from the hub to the outer edges of the web. Next, the spider created the temporary spiral shown in white. Finally, it went to work on the trap line shown in blue.

spinning threads that run from this **hub** to the outer edges of the web. These new threads look like the spokes on a bicycle wheel. The spider also adds a few **frame lines** to the outside of the web.

Now that the web's framework is secure, the spider returns to the hub. It makes the web more stable by spinning a temporary spiral of thread outward from the center.

Next, the spider moves to the outer edge of the web and begins adding **trap line**. This sticky silk slowly spirals inward toward the hub. When the spider reaches the temporary thread, it eats the silk and replaces it with trap line.

The spider stops laying trap line before it reaches the hub. It covers the center of the web with thick, zigzagging bands of dry thread. Scientists think these patterns may make the web more visible to birds, so they will not fly into it.

When the web is finally done, the spider waits. If the little arachnid is lucky, it will not be long until an unsuspecting insect gets snagged.

 Activity

On a warm, summer afternoon, take a walk in a local park. Hunt for spiderwebs on the ground, in bushes, and between trees. How many do you see? Do you see the spiders that made them? Write down all your observations in a notebook. Be sure to note the location of each web and the time you see it. Can you tell which kind of web it is?

Return to the park early the next morning. How many of the webs are still there? Do you see any new ones? Write down all your observations in a notebook.

If you would like to take photographs of the webs, pour talcum powder into an old sock before you leave home. When you see a web, gently shake the sock over the web. A thin layer of powder should fall onto the web. The powder will make the web easier to see in photographs.

 Glossary

abdomen—The back section of an insect's body.

anchor point—The lowest point of the spiderweb. The thread attached to the anchor point forms part of the web's framework.

arachnid—A group of small animals with two main body parts, a hard outer covering, and eight legs. Ticks, mites, scorpions, and spiders are all arachnids.

bridge line—The thick, strong thread from which a spiderweb hangs.

carnivore—An animal that hunts other animals and eats their meat, or flesh.

cephalothorax—The front part of an arachnid's body.

fibroin—The material from which spider silk is made.

frame line—A thread along the outer edge of a spiderweb that provides support.

funnel web—A sheet web with a structure in the middle or on the edge where spiders can hide.

hub—The center of a spiderweb.

nutrient—A substance that keeps the body of a living organism healthy.

orb web—A complicated, orderly spiderweb built high off the ground.

predator—An animal that hunts and kills other animals for food.

prey—An animal that is hunted by a predator.

sheet web—A flat spiderweb that is built close to the ground.

species—A group of similar creatures that can mate and produce healthy young.

spinneret—A tubelike structure on a spider's abdomen that releases silk.

tangled web—A spiderweb made of messy, crisscrossing silk strands close to the ground.

thorax—The middle section of an insect's body. The legs and wings are attached to the thorax.

trap line—A sticky thread in a spiderweb that traps, or catches, prey.

vibrate—To shake.

# Find Out More

BOOKS

Berger, Melvin. *Spinning Spiders*. New York: HarperCollins, 2003.

Markle, Sandra. *Spiders, Biggest! Littlest!* Honesdale, PA: Boyds Mills Press, 2004.

Murawski, Darlyne A. *Spiders and Their Webs*. Washington, D.C.: National Geographic, 2004.

WEB SITES

How Do Spiders Spin Their Webs?
www.coolquiz.com/trivia/explain/docs/spider.asp

Spider Silk
www.backyardnature.net/spidsilk.htm

Index

Page numbers for illustrations are in **boldface.**